OUT OF → THIS WORLD

A. LOH-HAGAN

T0102317

THEORY OF
TIME TRAVEL

45TH PARALLEL PRESS

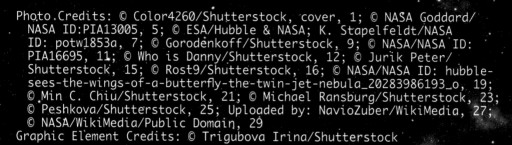

Published in the United States of America
by Cherry Lake Publishing
Ann Arbor, Michigan
www.cherrylakepublishing.com

Reading Adviser: Marla Conn, MS, Ed.,
   Literacy specialist, Read-Ability, Inc.
Book Designer: Jessica Rogner

Photo Credits: © Color4260/Shutterstock, cover, 1; © NASA Goddard/
   NASA ID:PIA13005, 5; © ESA/Hubble & NASA; K. Stapelfeldt/NASA
   ID: potw1853a, 7; © Gorodenkoff/Shutterstock, 9; © NASA/NASA ID:
   PIA16695, 11; © Who is Danny/Shutterstock, 12; © Jurik Peter/
   Shutterstock, 15; © Rost9/Shutterstock, 16; © NASA/NASA ID: hubble-
   sees-the-wings-of-a-butterfly-the-twin-jet-nebula_20283986193_o, 19;
   © Min C. Chiu/Shutterstock, 21; © Michael Ransburg/Shutterstock, 23;
   © Peshkova/Shutterstock, 25; Uploaded by: NavioZuber/WikiMedia, 27;
   © NASA/WikiMedia/Public Domain, 29
Graphic Element Credits: © Trigubova Irina/Shutterstock

45th Parallel Press is an imprint of
Cherry Lake Publishing Group

Library of Congress Cataloging-in-Publication Data
Names: Loh-Hagan, Virginia, author. | Loh-Hagan, Virginia.
   Out of this world.
Title: Theory of time travel / by Virginia Loh-Hagan.
Description: Ann Arbor, Michigan : Cherry Lake Publishing, [2020] |
   Series: Out of this world | Includes bibliographical references
   and index.
Identifiers: LCCN 2020006931 (print) | LCCN 2020006932 (ebook) |
   ISBN 9781534169258 (hardcover) | ISBN 9781534170933 (paperback) |
   ISBN 9781534172777 (pdf) | ISBN 9781534174610 (ebook)
Subjects: LCSH: Time travel--Juvenile literature. | Space and time-
   Juvenile literature. | Wormholes (Physics)-Juvenile literature.
Classification: LCC QB209.5 .L65 2020 (print) | LCC QB209.5 (ebook) |
   DDC 530.11--dc23
LC record available at https://lccn.loc.gov/2020006931
LC ebook record available at https://lccn.loc.gov/2020006932

Printed in the United States of America | Corporate Graphics

WHAT IS THE UNIVERSE?

The universe is huge. It's everything that exists. This includes planets, stars, and outer space. It includes living things on Earth.

The universe contains billions of galaxies. Galaxies are huge space collections. Galaxies are made up of billions of stars, gas, and dust. Galaxies include **solar** systems. Solar means sun. Earth is in the Milky Way galaxy. Galaxies spin in space. They spin very fast. There's a lot of space between stars and galaxies. This space is filled with dust, light, heat, and rays.

Before the birth of the universe, there was no time, space, or matter. Anything that takes up space is matter. Matter can exist in different states. The common states include solid, liquid, and gas. This is why things like air and smoke are considered matter. But the heat and light from a fire aren't matter. These don't take up space.

The universe hasn't always been the same size. It also hasn't always existed. Some scientists believe it began with a "big bang."

About 7 new stars are "born" each year in the Milky Way.

This is a **theory**. Theory means an idea. This theory explains how the universe was born. First, the universe was a super tiny blob, smaller than a pinhead! Then, that super tiny blob exploded. This happened 13.8 billion years ago. Next, energy spread out. Energy is made from matter. For example, the flames in a fire are matter. They take up space. But the heat you feel and the light you see from the flames are energy. Last, stars and planets formed. This all happened in less than a second.

Scientists think the universe is still expanding. Expanding means growing or spreading out. Scientists also think this expanding process is speeding up.

CHAPTER ONE

WHAT IS SPACE-TIME?

Time is **relative**. Relative means something has meaning only in relation to something else. Earth space and outer space are **three-dimensional** (3D). 3D means having length, width, and height. Time is the fourth dimension. Space and time can't exist without each other. They exist as **space-time**. Any event that happens in the universe involves both space and time.

There are distortions in space-time. For example, time passes more slowly for objects in gravitational waves. Gravitational waves are invisible. They travel at the speed of light. Gravitational waves happen when something large moves at a very high speed. An example would be when 2 black holes merge to become one. Another example is when a large star explodes. These events cause invisible ripples, or distortions, in space.

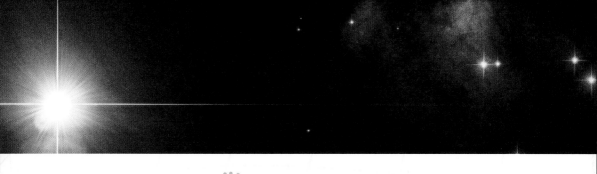

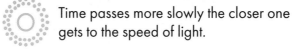

Time passes more slowly the closer one gets to the speed of light.

Some scientists study these distortions. They think these distortions support time travel. Time travel is traveling to the past or future. There's no proof of time travel. But there's some science to support it.

Dr. Albert Einstein developed the theory of special relativity. Time slows down or speeds up. This depends on how fast one moves relative to something else. For example, space objects travel at the speed of light. People inside a spaceship age more slowly than people on Earth. This effect is called **time dilation**. Time dilation is the slowing of time at high speeds.

Einstein also developed the theory of general relativity. Gravity is a force that pulls things toward a planet's ground. It affects the shape of space. It affects the flow of time. It causes movements in space. Space objects bend space-time. This bending brings distant points closer. It makes objects move on curved paths. These curves are caused by gravity.

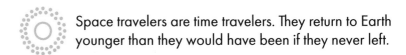

Space travelers are time travelers. They return to Earth younger than they would have been if they never left.

AMONG THE STARS: WOMEN IN SCIENCE

Jodie Whittaker was born in 1982. She's an English actress. In 2018, she became the first woman to play the Doctor in *Doctor Who*. She's the 13th person to play this role. *Doctor Who* is a science-fiction TV series. The Doctor is a Time Lord. The character is an alien who looks human. They are from the planet Gallifrey. They travel through time and space in a TARDIS. The TARDIS is a time machine. It stands for Time And Relative Dimension In Space. The Doctor is remade into a new body when they die. Whittaker is the newest Doctor. She told fans not to be afraid of her gender. She said, "Being a woman is who I am. And with this part, being a woman has less relevance than any other part I've played, except for that monumental historical moment of being the first woman Doctor ... Being the first female Doctor and showing children that their heroes in shows don't always look the same is a huge honor for me."

CHAPTER TWO

HOW DO BLACK HOLES SUPPORT TIME TRAVEL?

Black holes have all kinds of space and time distortions. They move fast. They have strong gravity. Gravity pulls on space and time. These are good conditions for traveling to the future.

Black holes are dense areas in space. They make deep gravity sinks. The deeper the gravity sinks, the more space distorts and curves. The gravity of black holes pulls so much in that nothing escapes. The boundary of black holes is called the "event horizon."

This is the point of no return. Matter can get in. But it can't get out. The closer to the event horizon, the slower time moves. But this is risky. Crossing the boundary means ceasing to exist.

The closest black hole to Earth is about 3,000 light-years away. Light-years describe the distance that light travels in a year.

The easiest way to time travel is to go fast. Some black holes move and travel at 5 million miles (8 million kilometers) an hour. Some people could use this speed. They could circle a black hole. They'd do this many times. They'd experience half the time of people far away from the black hole. They'd be in the future. For example, a person could circle a black hole for 5 years. On Earth, 10 years would have passed. Returning to Earth, that person would only be 5 years older! While everyone else aged 10 years. However, there are many risks. First, it'd be hard to avoid falling into the black hole. Second, space travel is dangerous.

 Some scientists think exceeding light speed could push people to travel back in time.

DOWN-TO-EARTH EXPERIMENT

Want to tell time without using a clock? Try out this experiment! Create your own sundial. Think like a scientist!

Materials:

- Cardboard
- Pencil
- Ruler
- Scissors
- Drinking straw
- Tape
- Magnetic compass
- Rock
- Alarm (clock or phone)

Instructions:

1. Use the cardboard's long side. This will be your sundial's bottom.

2. Make a small hole on the center of the long side of your cardboard. Make sure it's 2 inches (5 centimeters) from the bottom.

3. Make 3 small vertical cuts from the straw's bottom. Spread sections out flat.

4. Insert straw's top through the cardboard hole. Stop when you get to the cut sections. Secure the cut sections to the bottom of the cardboard. Use tape. Find a place where the sun shines all day. Place the cardboard straw-side up on a flat surface.

5. Use a compass to find north. Position the cardboard so the straw's shadow lines up with north. Secure cardboard to flat surface. Use tape or a heavy rock.

6. Set an alarm for the next top hour, like 12:00 or 1:00. Then, align the ruler with the straw's shadow. Trace the line and write down the time. Do this at the top of each hour.

As day goes on, Earth spins on its axis. The sun's rays will reach the sundial from different angles. This makes the straw cast shadows in different places. This sundial is only accurate for your location and time of year.

CHAPTER THREE

COULD WORMHOLES BE USED FOR TIME TRAVEL?

Scientists don't think anyone could escape from black holes. But they have theories about **wormholes**. Wormholes are tunnels. They go through space and time. They connect one black hole to another. Some people think wormholes are ways to travel from one galaxy to another. Some people think wormholes can be used for time travel.

Wormholes are formed in black holes. Gravity is strongest at a black hole's center. The center is known as **singularity**. The singularity is a point. It's a place of **infinitely** dense matter. Infinite means having no limits. Singularity slows down time. It points to the future.

 As people move toward singularity, they'll be stretched out. They'll be "spaghettified." This means being stretched out like a spaghetti noodle.

Black holes **rotate**. Rotate means to spin. The singularity could also rotate. They could rotate really fast. They could become rings instead of points. Ring singularities bend and twist space and time. These rings could serve as doors.

But there's a problem for time travelers. There's no proof of wormholes. Some scientists think wormholes could be found in **quantum foam**. Quantum foam is the universe's smallest environment. Tiny wormholes may blink in and out of existence. For moments, they could link space and time. These wormholes would be too small and brief for human time travel. If they exist, scientists could learn to make them bigger and more stable. This would require a lot of energy.

The wormholes in quantum foam would be smaller than atoms.

IT'S (ALMOST) ROCKET SCIENCE

Flying to space is hard. The spaceship's distance from Earth needs to be figured out. Space navigators are people who direct paths in space. They send signals to spaceships. Spaceships return signals to Earth. The time it takes for the signals to travel is the spaceship's distance from Earth. This signal travels at the speed of light. Navigators figure out space destinations. They send many signals. They take many measurements over time. They use this data to calculate where spaceships are and where they're headed. To do this, navigators need accurate and stable clocks. The Deep Space Atomic Clock (DSAC) was launched in space in 2019. It saves lots of time. It lets spaceships independently travel in space. This way, spaceships don't need to wait to get information from Earth. The DSAC is the first clock stable enough to map a spaceship's path. It's also small enough to be inside of a spaceship.

CHAPTER FOUR

WHAT ARE COSMIC STRINGS?

Time moves forward. It doesn't move backward. But there's a theory about cosmic strings. This theory could be used to travel back in time. There's no proof cosmic strings exist. But many scientists believe they do.

After the "big bang," the universe cooled. It may have cooled too quickly. This quick cooling created cracks in the universe. These cracks exist in space-time. They're rips and tears in the universe.

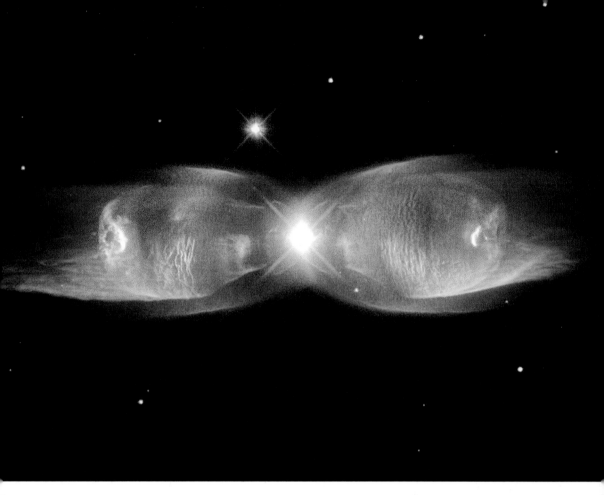

 J. Richard Gott introduced the idea that cosmic strings could allow time travel.

They're called cosmic strings. Cosmic strings are stretched across the universe. They're tubes of pure energy. They have huge amounts of energy. They're heavy. They have a lot of pressure. They're thinner than atoms. They're invisible. They're light-years long.

Cosmic strings are infinite, or in loops. They have no end and no beginning point. They can go on forever. They have strong gravitational pulls. As 2 strings get close, they pull strongly on each other. They wiggle. They form loops. They can bend space-time. They could be used for time travel. A spaceship could loop around cosmic strings. It'd follow a curved path. It'd travel at quick speeds. It could travel to the past. But there's a danger. Using cosmic strings could cause a black hole.

 Traveling back in time 1 year would take half the energy of an entire galaxy.

CHAPTER FIVE

HOW WOULD TIME MACHINES WORK?

Most scientists agree that time machines are needed for time travel. Time machines are like cars. They **transport** people to the past and future. Transport means to travel.

Time machines need a lot of energy. They need **exotic matter**. Exotic matter is different from normal matter. It has opposite energy. It doesn't obey the laws of gravity. It moves in the opposite direction of normal matter. There's no physical proof this matter exists.

Scientists could build time-traveling spaceships. These spaceships would need to travel at the speed of light. They'd need a lot of energy. They could use antimatter. Antimatter is the opposite of regular matter. When antimatter and matter meet, they destroy each other. This crash creates enough energy to fuel spaceships.

 Wormholes use negative energy.

Scientists have been working on time machines. They use science and math. They also use their imagination.

The Tipler time machine is also called the Tipler **Cylinder**. Cylinders are tubes. Tipler's time machine would need matter that's 10 times the sun's mass. Mass is the amount of matter in something. It'd roll this matter into a long, dense tube. It'd spin a few billion times. A spaceship would follow an exact path around this tube. This tube is like a black hole.

Tipler's time machine might not ever be made. The tube would need to be infinitely long. Matter that strong would be hard to get.

 According to experts, we probably would only be able to travel back in time, not forward.

CHAPTER SIX

WHO STUDIED TIME TRAVEL?

Dr. Albert Einstein lived from 1879 to 1955. He studied **physics**. Physics is the science of matter and energy. Einstein is thought to be one of the greatest minds. Time travel research is based on his theories. His theories and math equations served as the starting points. Equations are math statements. They explain ideas.

Dr. Kurt Godel lived from 1906 to 1978. He studied math. He was Einstein's friend. He worked on Einstein's theory of relativity. He showed that time travel was a mathematical possibility.

 Before he was 15, Einstein mastered calculus. Most students take calculus for the first time in college!

He said a rotating universe would support time travel. The universe would create loops in time. People could go along the loop. They could go back in time.

Stephen Hawking was a famous scientist. He studied physics. In 2009, Hawking hosted a party for time travelers. He didn't send invites until after it happened. No one came. Hawking said this was proof time travel didn't exist. He also said, "The best evidence we have that time travel is not possible, and never will be, is that we have not been invaded by hordes of tourists from the future."

He used current science to disprove time travel. But he was open to the idea of time travel in the future. It's up to future scientists to see what's possible.

 Stephen Hawking's friends nicknamed him "Einstein."

CYLINDER (SIL-uhn-dur) tube

EXOTIC MATTER (ig-ZAH-tik MAT-ur) matter that deviates from normal matter

INFINITELY (IN-fuh-nit-lee) without an end or limits

PHYSICS (FIZ-iks) science of matter and energy

QUANTUM FOAM (KWAN-tum FOHM) the universe's smallest environment

RELATIVE (REL-uh-tiv) something having meaning only in relation to something else

ROTATE (ROH-tate) to spin

SINGULARITY (sing-gyuh-LAR-ih-tee) the center of a black hole

SOLAR (SOH-lur) relating to the sun

SPACE-TIME (SPAYS TIME) a mathematical model that joins space and time into a single idea called a continuum

THEORY (THEER-ee) an idea meant to explain something

THREE-DIMENSIONAL (three-duh-MEN-shuh-nuhl) having length, width, and height

TIME DILATION (TIME dye-LAY-shuhn) the slowing of time at high speeds

TRANSPORT (TRANS-port) to travel

WORMHOLES (WURM-holez) tunnels through space and time that connect one black hole to another

FAR-OUT FACTS

- Charlotte Anne Moberly and Eleanor Jourdain were school leaders at St. Hugh's College in United Kingdom. In 1911, they wrote a book. They believed they traveled through time. They went to the Palace of Versailles. They were in the gardens. They were transported to the 18th century. They thought they saw Queen Marie Antoinette. Some people believed them. But most people didn't.

- Chronesthesia is the brain's ability to have awareness of past and future. Certain brain areas are more active when remembering the past and envisioning the future. Animals don't have chronesthesia like we do. Human babies don't have chronesthesia because they're too young.

LEARN MORE

Pohlen, Jerome. *Albert Einstein and Relativity for Kids: His Life and Ideas with 21 Activities and Thought Experiments.* Chicago, IL: Chicago Review Press, 2012.

Tyson, Neil deGrasse. *StarTalk: Everything You Ever Need to Know About Space Travel, Sci-Fi, the Human Race, the Universe, and Beyond.* Washington, DC: National Geographic, 2017.

Tyson, Neil deGrasse, with Gregory Mone. *Astrophysics for Young People in a Hurry.* New York, NY: Norton Young Readers, 2019.

INDEX

ABOUT THE AUTHOR

Dr. Virginia Loh-Hagan is an author, university professor, and former classroom teacher. If she could time travel, she'd go to a future where she can eat hot dogs without gaining weight. She lives in San Diego, California, with her very tall husband and very naughty dogs.